PARENTING UNCUT

Parenting Uncut

A manual for parents of 2 - 4.99 year olds

Copyright © 2019 N Taylor. All rights reserved.
ISBN 978-0-6488642-2-6

All In This Book!

Seven Things You Need to Know Before You Give Birth	7
How Long it Will Take You to Do Things With a Young Child	10
Fiction, Deception, And Lack of Parental Christmas Spirit	19
Stuff My Toddler Carries Around	21
"They Don't Come With a Manual". (Says who?)	25
When You Have a Kid Who's Not Like You	28
Oh, The Agony of Toddler Mealtimes	32
Let it Go. Just Let it Go.	38
Hello. I'm Officially a Dance Mum now.	43
On Having a Second….Or More	47
The Awesomeness of iEntertainment	48
Keeping Your Child Amused	52
Toilet Training	55
Milestones. WTF are they?	61
Other People Will Feed Your Children Sugar	68
Mothers' Groups: The Virtual Kind	72
Dear Parenting Expert	76
Things You Said You'd Never Do When You Had a Kid	80
Things You Find Yourself Saying After You Have a Kid	85
Things You Find Yourself Doing After You Have a Kid	86
#hashtag	87
Twitterism	92
The Dearth of Good Childrens' Movies	101
The Other Great Thing About Caesarians	105
My Little Pony and Other Obsessions	106
Preschool and Beyond	110
Some Useful Statistics	113

Preface

Once you discover you're pregnant with your first and start telling everyone about it, people will delight in terrorizing you about the newborn stage. Even those who've never parented! Apparently, you'll never sleep a full night again. Your baby will cry for no obvious reason and you'll go mad trying to stop it. You'll be constantly covered in baby sick, you won't have enough time to take a shower on a daily basis, your cups of tea will go cold and you won't remember where you've put them anyway, and leaving the house will be impossible for about 8 months unless you have an entourage to carry all your baby stuff for you.

But no one will warn you about once they grow out of that sweet, loveable, *easy*, stage. It's like everyone who ever had a kid has managed to block the toddler through to preschool ages from their memory, and once you make it that far yourself, you understand why.

This book is dedicated to keeping the sanity of the parents of two to 4.99 year olds intact. It's to help you feel that you are not alone; you are normal, and so is your kid. Sometimes, that's all you need to know.

A is for....

Answers

You won't have any. When your child asks you "Where does my friend Sadie live?" and "Why is a rainbow?" and "Mummy, what is that blinking light on your dashboard?" you won't know how to answer. You didn't even know your kid had a friend called Sadie.

You can either say "I don't know, honey", which will be deeply unsatisfactory to your child, or you can think on your feet and make something up. Or you can flip the question on its arse and say "Gosh, honey, what do YOU think that flashing light on my dashboard is?" She might tell you, and then you'll both know.

Seven things you need to know before you give birth (so it might be too late)

The terrible twos will use every bit of patience you ever had, and then you'll run out of it.

I had so little experience of children before I had one that I thought they only had their terrible two tantrums at shopping centres. I thought I'd just avoid the whole problem by not taking my child to Woolworths until she turned five. Turns out the *only* place my child has never chucked a narney is at a shopping centre. The place where she lost it most often and most extremely during the terrible twos, was at home with me alone. And there was nothing I could do about that except take her to Kmart and Woolies as often as possible. I became a person who hated grocery shopping to one who purposely made it a three times weekly outing, to last as long as possible. (PS. Other righteous parents will tell you their two year old isn't so bad. Talk to them again when their child is three).

You will sound like your mother, even as you try so very hard not to.

You will completely understand why your mother said everything she said, and you will repeat these things over and over. Some of my favourites: I'm waiting. Stop playing with your food and eat your dinner. Don't you make me come in there. I'm leaving without you. Go back to bed now. Put your shoes on. How many times do I have to tell you? How many times have I told you? I don't care if you don't eat dinner, but you won't be getting dessert. Hurry up. Do you need to go to the toilet? Are you sure? What did your last slave die of? Speaking of which.....

You will feel like a slave pretty much every minute you are with your child.

I'm not very good at being a slave. It makes me a bit surly sometimes, I'm ashamed to admit. Especially when I don't get thanked and I've had to do a particular task just to get someone to stop screaming at me. Part of me thinks I shouldn't respond to such behaviour, and the other part is just so desperate for peace that I'll do anything. This conundrum does contribute to the general insanity of parenthood.

Your child will be an angel for their grandparents.

Get very used to hearing "oh really? But s/he never behaves like that here". You'll beg your child to throw just one really huge meltdown at nanny's, for proof. Please. But of course, they won't.

Your life will be Groundhog Day.

I know I'm not alone here. In a poll on Facebook where people were asked to nominate a movie that is their life with a toddler, this movie title came up many times. I love the movie. I don't always love living it.

Your cushions will spend so much time on the floor.

And you'll spend so much time picking them up you'll contemplate just getting rid of them. Your child will start to throw all the cushions they can find onto the floor, from the age of about 15 months, give or take 5 months. And it will continue to last until they are three years old, when they will continue to throw the cushions on the floor but then extend that into creating forts and beds for their dollies. I don't know when it stops because I'm still waiting.

It will take you so, so long to get out of the house, you'll have to start doing it the night before.

How children can waste so much time doing anything but what they are supposed to be doing is quite remarkable. And while you're asking them for the 57th time to come into their room so you can put on their shoes, they'll be singing at the top of their voices and therefore ignoring you. They should write a book about procrastination. They are experts.

B is for....

Bribery

I paid my child to get dressed this morning, and to my stunned surprise, it worked. Do what you have to do.

How long it will take you to do things with a young child

*All times are approximate and represent the minimum recommended allowance

ACTION	GENERAL GUIDELINE
Leave the house	From 10 to 45 minutes Depending on how much stuff you've got to carry, whether your child has been to the toilet in the last 35 minutes, the weather, how busy your street is, whether there are flowers to pick in your next door neighbour's yard, whether there is a small item in your child's shoe that you can't see, and how dangerous it would be if your child got away from you onto the street. Note: add an extra 15 minutes for each extra child.
Get your child into the car	From 5 to 25 minutes Depending on what kind of car seat you have, how tight the straps are, whether your child is wearing a princess dress and how many layers of tulle there are, how thirsty your child is and what mood your child is in.
Get your child out of the car	From 2 to 17 minutes Depending on whether they can step down from the seat themselves (which will add time), how many tags are on the car seat and which text they'd like read to them, how many buttons on the dashboard they'd like explained, how late you are arriving to your destination, and what mood your child is in.

ACTION	GENERAL GUIDELINE
Get your child dressed	From 5 to 90 minutes Depending on the season/how many layers are required, whether they will wear a warm layer as it's mid-winter, the current fashion, your child's favourite colours, whether they will or will not wear denim today, whether they will or will not wear a dress today, if the clothes they wore yesterday are in the wash covered in mud and they only want those clothes, if wearing socks hurts their toes, if they decide they want to dress themselves (will add at least 30 minutes) or if they decide after finally becoming fully dressed that they want to change into something completely different.
Get your child undressed	From 5 to 36 minutes Depending on whether you have run a bath for them which will get slowly colder as you wait for them to undress or let you undress them, what you've got cooking on the stove for dinner and how easily it will burn unsupervised, whether you have a dog or cat that will get into the pot while you're not watching, whether your child wanted bubbles when you started running the bath but now doesn't want them at all, how much sand comes out of their shoes, socks, pockets and sleeves that you have to quickly clean up before it is run all through the house.

ACTION	GENERAL GUIDELINE
Get your child into a bath	1 to 22 minutes You might think this is the easy part, because they are naked and all you have to do is lift them in. Nah. You'll have to chase them all over the house first. And if the bath is too hot (despite it being tepid) you'll have to wait another 6 minutes before they will put in more than a toe without screaming. And as soon as they get in there, they'll need to go to the toilet.
Get your child out of a bath	1 to 10 minutes Again, you just lift them out, right? Well, it really depends on how slippery they are and if they can get away from you. I find that if I pretend to lift up the plug, my child will immediately stand up and beg to be lifted out, because she's afraid she'll go down the drain with the bathwater. I've no idea where she got this idea, but I don't deny it. That's a free tip for you.
Get your child into bed	10-300 minutes We've been really, really lucky with this one. Our average time for this one is about 15 minutes; on a really good night, 10 minutes and a bad night, about 45. Some parents will burst into tears when they hear it only takes three stories, seven cuddles and kisses, one trip to the toilet and 45 minutes maximum to get our child to sleep. When we say there isn't even crying involved on the majority of nights they will want to choke us. If it takes you over 2 hours to get your kid to sleep, my thoughts are with you. I don't know how you cope.

ACTION	GENERAL GUIDELINE
Brush your child's teeth	5 to 23 minutes Depending on which toothbrush they want to use (because they never want to part with a used toothbrush, so you'll end up with 16 in the cup), how many questions they want answered before they'll open their mouth for a toothbrush, how many things they forgot to tell you about their day, how the toothpaste tastes, how long they'll let you brush for before insisting on doing it themselves, whether they spit water all over their pajama top then scream because it's wet.
Brush your child's hair	0 to 18 minutes Zero because you might not bother if you decide it's too hard; up to eight depending on how long and knotty your child's hair is and whether it needs to be pulled into an elastic, whether there is still an elastic in there somewhere from yesterday, whether they'll let you do it while they are eating breakfast (bonus points for being clever there), whether you use a detangling spray and if so, whether it smells nice or yucky.
Get a picture of your child smiling	1 minute to never Sad but true. Unless you consider one of those gruesome baring-all-my-teeth snarly sort of photos "smiling". I don't.

ACTION	GENERAL GUIDELINE
Get your child to eat their dinner	30 to 120 minutes. It still amazes me that I have to beg my child to eat. In my whole life, I have never been told to eat my dinner. What is it with kids these days? Do they live on air and sun, like windowsill plant pots? Or do they just eat anything but mummy's cooking? How can anyone spend up to two hours looking at a plate of perfectly tasty dinner (periodically getting up from the table to run about like a headless chicken) and not eat any of it? And then scream because you won't give them dessert?
Drop your child off at daycare/ preschool	5 to 25 minutes. There are so many factors here, but the most important one is how easily your child can be distracted by something that's fun by their educator while you slip out the door. The whole scenario can also change from day to day, so don't get lulled into a false sense of security when your child says goodbye happily for 25 days in a row. The 26th time will be a screaming mess.
Collect your child from daycare/ preschool	5 to 25 minutes. Correlated to how long it takes to drop them off. The sadder they were when you left them in the morning, the harder it is to drag them out at the end of the day.
Get your child to answer a question	1 minute to never The irony. They are full of questions but almost no answers. And don't bother asking how their day was at preschool, because they don't want to talk about it. Ok?

C is for....

Cake Smash

There are lots of little rituals you find out about when you join the parenting world, and one of these is to buy a really beautiful expensive cake for your child's first birthday, sit them in front of it, and let them demolish it with their bare hands, smearing it all over themselves, the floor and the dog. You must hire a professional photographer to capture this and get one photo blown up, framed and hung on the wall.

It is at this point that some parents discover that their child despises getting icing on their fingers.

D is for....

Drama

If you have girls, be prepared for this. (Although I have heard of boy drama queens too). There will be a lot of drama.

Everything is a big deal, such as if you try to make them wear a top to bed that has a little smudge of paint on it. Or when you cut up their pieces of chicken dinner and you make the pieces too small. Or too large. Or you ask them to do something you know they can do, like take off their shoes, and thus ensues an epic meltdown. You get the idea.

Fiction, Deception, And Lack of Parental Christmas Spirit

Okay. I am one of Those Parents.

Here it is. I won't ever be telling my daughter that Santa Claus is real. I will have to give her a very simple explanation about him, because he's everywhere in December and we won't be able to escape him, but I plan to tell her that he is just a character from story books like Hey Duggie and Peppa Pig. The real giver of presents in our house is mummy and daddy, who love you and work reasonably hard to pay for all the stuff you get just for being our kid.

I still remember the real confusion about Santa when I was a very small child. My parents told me he was real, and drummed up a lot of excitement about delivery of presents and the importance of good behaviour, and so on. But I was always a bit suspicious. Why were there so many Santas in shopping centres? One on every floor of every store? How did one man manage to deliver all those presents? I didn't know how many children there were in the world, but there seemed to be a lot just in my school. How did that sleigh actually fly, and what if you didn't have a chimney? Why did Santa look a bit different in every drawing, photo, movie and cartoon?

I was a little dismayed and maybe a bit relieved when I discovered the truth - to be honest as I'd never quite believed in him, the reality was not unexpected - but the real disappointment was squarely with my parents, who had lied to me all these years! And that's why I'm not going to lie about Santa. We lie to our children enough as it is, just to get through the day with as few meltdowns as possible (eg. I'll drive off without you of you don't get in this car right now. I'm usually lying when I say that.)

When she asks, she'll hear the truth. And that goes for the tooth fairy as well.

Stuff My Toddler Carries Around

This is a photo of what my two year old carried with her for a couple of hours today.

It's a balloon, a stripey neck pillow and a packet of 32 pink decorative fluffy balls from Daiso. It made getting her in and out of the car a few times quite an interesting little challenge.

The stuff she also wanted to bring on our visit, which I managed to wrangle out of her tiny hands at the front door, were: her other balloon, three used toothbrushes, a drumstick and a small soft toy in the shape of a cat head.

It's all very charming that she's a mobile hoarder. I don't even know how she manages to get it all in her grasp, especially with those little hands. I should buy her a big shopping bag, or maybe a trolley like the little old ladies use. But that might just encourage her further.

When I was her age I absolutely HAD to have my pillow with me. It wasn't a regular pillow, but a small one I could tuck under my arm. If I left the house without someone making sure I had it, there was apparent hell to pay. My parents bought dozens of replacements of this breed of pillow over the years. They speak of it fondly, as though it was a really cute and adorable little habit, but when I insist that it must have driven them crazy, they do quickly admit that it did.

At least when mini-me leaves the house it's always with something different, so if something gets lost she doesn't care. That's got to be preferable to having an emotional attachment to a pillow.

> Miss Three: Can I have a bedtime story?
>
> Me: Sure, honey. I was so proud of you today. You played beautifully with mummy's friend's little girls and you shared nicely. You didn't get upset when of them snatched a toy from you and wouldn't let you play with it. You didn't throw any tantrums and did as you were told. You were happy and lovely. I love you very much.
>
> Her: Can I have a different story?

E is for....

Eh

Sometimes my parenting style is "sure". Sometimes it's "over my dead body". Sometimes it's "WTF?" And sometimes it's just "eh". It's on these days that I'm at my happiest. It's my version of "Om" and I didn't have to do yoga to get there.

"They Don't Come With a Manual". (Says who?)

When you get pregnant, someone will say to you at some point that "the baby doesn't come with a manual". Oh really?

There are so many places you can go to find limitless information on getting pregnant, pregnancy, birth, newborns, babies, toddlers and so on, right up till your child is no longer in your care. Here are a few sources of information.

Your local library.
Mummy blogs.
Online forums.
Facebook mothers' groups.
Real life mothers' groups.
Friends and family.
Anyone who ever had a baby.

(You can even use plain old Google, although some would say researching for medical advice on Dr Google isn't always the best idea.)

It's a dead cert that any problem you've experienced throughout parenthood or pre-parenthood, has been experienced by at least 985 other people who happen to be online right now, 47 of them usually on a local Facebook mothers' group. And if it's not exactly your problem, it'll be close enough.

Also, sometimes you just need a bit of a rant more than actual advice. For example, I could very easily rant about how my two year old hates, with a passion, being lifted into her high chair for a meal, and will make herself very heavy and unliftable three times a day, accompanying this trick with a high pitched screech, kicking and flailing, just to make it extra fun for me. (She doesn't do this when we are about to do some painting. Oh no. That's apparently much more pleasurable than eating.)

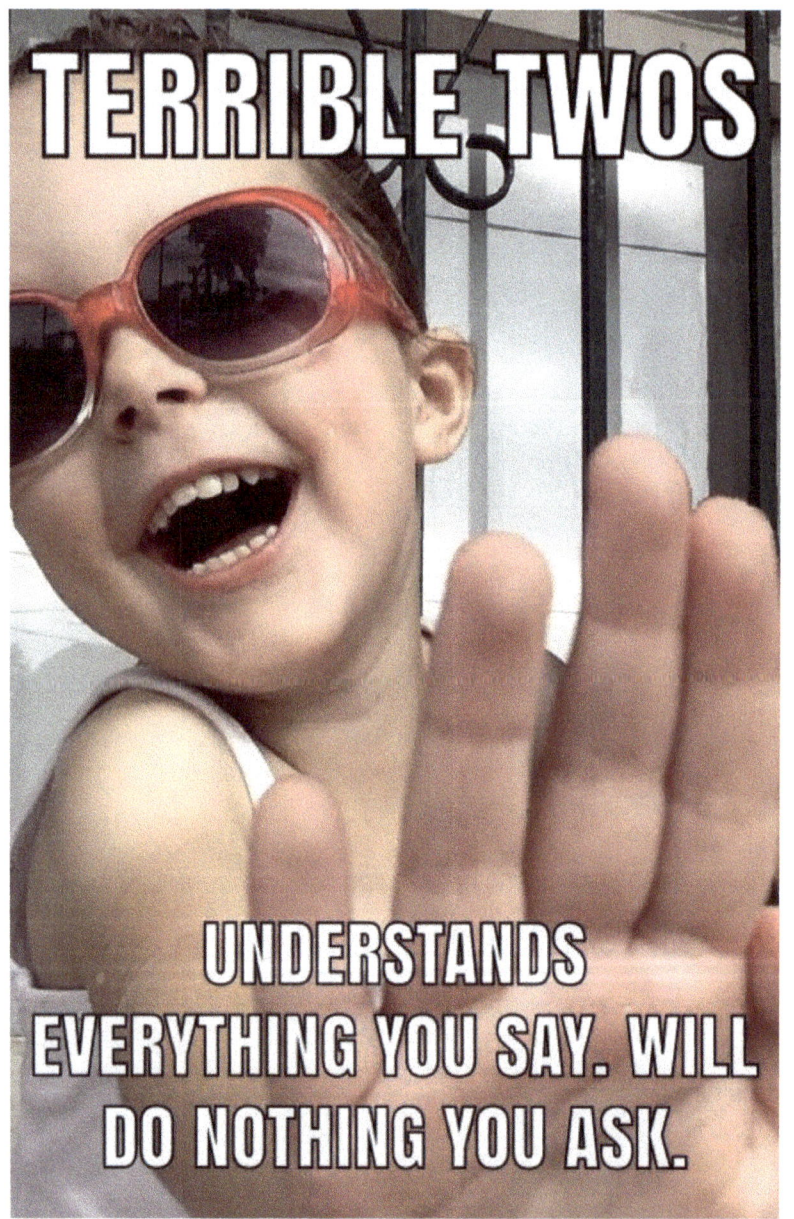

I read 150 books about babies before I had one and none of them mentioned this joyful habit, so I don't know when it will end, but if I was really worried about it I'd post on Facebook. Those 47 people would chime in within 36 minutes in total solidarity, and we'd all have a great big whinge and it'd feel great. The truth is, I don't even need to do it. Some of the things I read about parenthood make my battles seem very small indeed.

F is for....

Fathers' Day

Do you remember asking your dad what he wanted for Father's Day, and he used to say "a bit of bloody peace and quiet"? I used to wonder why he never wanted an actual gift.

Now I understand.

When you have a kid who's not like you

My child is, as my amused mum has commented, nothing like me.

My two year old gets up at 5:30am, ready to start the day.

I have NEVER done this unless there is a flight to catch. I didn't do it when I was two, or 22, and certainly not now. I keep asking my daughter why she does this but she never has a satisfactory answer for me.

She jumps up and down with excitement about everything and nothing.

As a child, I kept all unnecessary movement to a minimum. As a result, I was quite chubby until at least the age of two.

As a toddler, I used to sit and draw for hour upon hour.

My daughter is not generally interested in drawing. She is far more interested in taking all the lids off her textas, leaving them to suffocate in the open air, and putting all the lids on her fingers like talons. She will wear them like this all day, holding meltdowns when they have to come off for such things as eating and bathing. She did this repeatedly for months, long after I had thrown out the textas and kept the lids.

My daughter says hello to everyone

She greets random people walking down the street with a cheerful and slightly surprised sounding "hello!". As in, "fancy seeing you here!" No one fails to be amused by this. I on the other hand was crazy shy and wouldn't have done this if you'd paid me.

She's a joiner

All her classes – swimming, martial arts, dancing – she gets right in there in the middle of it and jumps up and down not caring who's standing next to her. She's not shy of other kids and won't hesitate to tell them about her new shoes. I used to cry during my swimming lessons, so the teacher would hold me the whole time and I didn't learn to swim until I was 22.

She's fussy about her attire

My clothing needs were simple as a toddler: pants only. No dresses. As long as I got that sorted, I was happy. But my daughter takes a different approach.

We try to avoid a morning battle before preschool by deciding on an ensemble before bed the night before. We have to consider almost every item in her (considerable) wardrobe before we can arrive at her choices. We flick through a dozen dresses, ten pairs of shoes, thirty pairs of socks. And that's after I've explained that we can't wear our winter clothes right now, nor the items that she is yet to grow into. After a good quarter hour, the clothes are laid neatly on the floor (by her) in the order in which she plans to dress. Even underwear requires careful deliberation: will it be Peppa Pig or Minnie Mouse tomorrow?

So what happens when she wakes? She puts everything on, and proudly comes to show me. And have you guessed what she says next?

"Mummy. I've changed my mind. I don't want to wear this anymore."

She doesn't feel the cold

My daughter fusses about having to wear sleeves or pant legs on the coldest of days. She'll grudgingly put a hoodie on before we leave the house, but as soon as we're outside she'll rip it off down to a t-shirt. I used to wear a cardigan everywhere I went, all year round. I was born 85.

She will not be bribed

I'm not so pleased about this one. I wish I could offer her something to persuade her to do what I need her to do. But she won't do anything unless she wants to, regardless of what food, entertainment or gifts are proffered. I wish she would accept bribery. Life would be easier.

She's very sporty

In primary school, I played D grade reserve netball. That means that they could have asked any other kid in school who'd never played netball before, and that kid would have done a better job of it than I. My daughter already has four sporting trophies at the age of four. I earned my first trophy at 35 (and it was from work. For accounting).

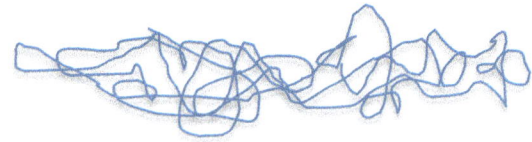

There is just one likeness to me that I see in her, and it's her propensity to line or stack objects neatly in rows or piles. Fridge magnets are a perfect example: she likes to line up all the magnets in a long straight row which suits me very well. (She also sometimes puts things away without being asked, which makes my heart burst. She's my daughter after all).

G is for....

Grandparents

I once caught my mum about to feed my daughter a piece of chocolate cake for lunch. I protested, and was given a look from my mother sour enough to shrivel an apple. Did she feed me like this when I was three?

No. She did not.

Oh, The Agony of Toddler Mealtimes

Here are the most frustrating scenes that are the pain of mealtimes with a three year old. Consider yourself warned.

The refusal to so much as sniff at anything put in front of them that's not bananas, yoghurt, bread or milk.

For the 65,000th time in a row, tonight I placed a delicious, healthy meal in front of my three year old. It wasn't too hot. It wasn't spicy. It didn't contain any of her least favourite foods, and there were just a few spoonfuls of it, so as not to overwhelm her with too much food. The reaction, for the 65,000th time, was to violently push the plate away and scream "NO". I must admit, I'm pretty sick of this. At least my husband said it was delicious. And I thought it was pretty good too. Should I be grateful that she at least doesn't throw the plate onto the floor any more, like she did when she was two?

The getting up from the table (or, clambering down from the chair) at least 9 times during the meal.

Why can't they just, you know, sit down and eat? Is eating such a chore? I've always enjoyed the sensation of soothing my hunger; both now and even as a child. Why must there be frenzied running about the room every 4 minutes?

The taking of an hour to eat a piece of bread

As my child basically eats bananas, yoghurt and bread right now, that's what I end up giving her when she spurns dinner every night. Must it take an hour to chew through a piece of bread?

The asking for a specific item of food, which is then ignored, or the asking for a second helping, which is then ignored

So much waste. I understand how mums just eat whatever their child hasn't eaten. Why bother cooking for yourself when you can live off leftovers? My child will eat Weetbix for breakfast, sometimes, but there are days when she asks for but does not eat them (I don't mind eating those) or ask for a second helping but does not eat them (I'm not crazy about eating stuff that's been added to an already dirty bowl. I'm not that kind of mother). I've taken to throwing into the plate a handful of crumbs from the bottom of the bag (you know; the crumbs you normally chuck out) as soon as I get that far into the pack, and calling that her breakfast. Is that wrong?

The calm acceptance and consumption of most food available at any location that's not home.

It gives you the irrits.

I've decided to start cooking whatever I feel like, stuff that I used to cook for my husband and myself that had actual spices in it. Stuff that had vegetables other than peas. Stuff that had meat in it, and tasty sauces. Because if she won't eat anything I cook, then why impose strict limits on our meals? I'm looking forward to cooking some yummy meals like the ones we used to have before ol' Miss Picky came along. I'll just have to stock up on bananas, yoghurt and bread.

H is for....

Hard Liquor

I don't drink. But I'm this close to starting it up.

The Three Year Old Mealtime Commandments

1. There shall be no green in the salad
2. There shall be no yellow in the salad
3. There shall be no red in the salad
4. There shall be no beany or sprouty things in the salad
5. There shall be no dressing on the salad
6. Actually, I won't be eating any salad
7. I will eat meat, as long as it's not lamb
8. I will eat meat, as long as it's not pork
9. I will eat meat, as long as it's not turkey
10. I will eat meat, as long as it's chicken
11. But I don't want any skin on the chicken
12. And I don't want any sauce on the chicken or on anything else ever
13. Actually I will eat any meat if it's in a sausage
14. Actually I will eat any meat if it's on your plate and you are really enjoying it
15. Can I have dessert yet?
16. I will eat vegetables if it's potato
17. But if the potato has any green herby bits on it I will scream and ask you to remove them
18. I will eat vegetables if it's peas
19. But first I will throw some on the table so daddy can say "you peed on the table!"
20. I will eat vegetables if it's broccoli
21. But only once so you can brag about it to your mummy friends and then I won't eat it any more
22. I will eat hidden vegetables such as grated carrot only as long as it's in a pasta dish with cheese sauce
23. If you try to hide any green vegetables such as zucchini in a cheesy pasta dish I will spot the green specks and call you out
24. After all the fuss, I will still expect dessert whether I eat my dinner or not

I is for....

Imagination

Your child will want to pretend lots of things, like they're a Smurf or a kitten or made of playdough, or that you're the baby and they're the daddy/mummy.

My favourite is when my child begs me to pretend she's invisible. I have to ignore everything she says and pretend I can't see her. It's great.

Let it go. Just let it go.

As the song says (yep, the Frozen one) and Kath Day-Knight wisely sighs, "let it go". I'm talking about my compulsive tendencies to extreme neatness and order, overflowing into my child's art and craft sessions.

I'm not going to label it as OCD, because that's a real and serious condition which although is often joked about, isn't what I'm dealing with here. But there must be a name for it. How can I describe my anxiety when my three year old decides to mix her playdough colours as she makes balls and biscuits? Slowly, the 8 different colour pots are beginning to resemble the same murky shade they are all destined to become. At first, the joining and kneading of colours produces a pretty marbling, which looks great as you roll it flat and cut into shapes. But even as a young child, I knew that effect was only temporary. My adventures in plasticine and playdough always ended with every colour back in its rightful tub. I realised after our first playdough session, after convincing her not to eat it, that my daughter's desire to keep colours apart was not strong.

Also, let's mention painting. In contrast to her liberal use of colour in playdough, my daughter will quite often insist on using just one colour when painting a masterpiece. It's usually blue. I plead with her to try other colours. She has 27 which I thought would be quite tempting. I offer to tip any or all of them onto the paper or palette for her to enjoy, but she often screams NOOOO JUST BLUE. Sometimes, she will grudgingly accept different colours. But then, like the playdough, they are all mixed up, usually by hand, to produce brown. I have this urge to interfere, but I have to restrain myself. It is her artwork after all.

It doesn't really matter what implements I give her to paint with, either. We have sponges, toothbrushes, stamps and of course paintbrushes. But she's really only interested in using her hands. And the painting quite quickly moves from the paper to her hands and entire arms. She's much more interested in giving them all a good coat of paint than the actual canvas. Funnily enough, I could get her to paint some wonderful things on paper and other surfaces when she was two. But now she's three, it's all about body paint. It's not nearly as satisfying (for me) as filing beautiful painted masterpieces in her art scrapbook.

We have a huge collection of textas and a whiteboard to draw upon, but I'm still waiting for my daughter to focus on using the actual textas to draw with, rather than murdering full sets of 10 by wearing the lids as talons. For now, surviving textas remain safely in storage until I think she's ready for correct usage.

I've slowly become more accepting and less interfering of these strange techniques in arts and craft. But I'm sure I'm not alone in this tendency of mine so I've decided to give it a name – "Creative Supervisory Stress Disorder (CSSD)". It's now officially a Thing.

J is for....

Justification

This is where you justify your parental behaviours to make you feel better about your parenting. It's totally normal and necessary for your sanity. Some examples:

It's ok for my child to play on their iPad for 6 hours, because it's raining and that's what you do on rainy days.

It's ok to tell my child that she has to play by herself for a while because she needs to learn valuable life skills. Like how she will deal with it when she doesn't have a date on a Saturday night.

It's fine for my kid to see me lose my shit once in a while (or... more often) because I'm tired of not being obeyed. They need to know how far they can push people so they can learn to stop being annoying little turds who no-one likes.

See?

Hello. I'm Officially a Dance Mum Now.

Here is a picture of my daughter while we were attempting to dress her for her first ever dance concert. Her objection, once we got past the wearing of the dance tights, was the wearing of her blue and red hair clips, so her father pinned her between his feet (those are the tops of his blue shoes) while I applied the clips. (This is the only way to get things done sometimes). Once the clips were in, there was no further fuss.

As a new dance mum I had no idea what to expect of a three year old on her first stage, and I'd spent the last two months joking with my fellow new dance mums that we would be lucky to even get our kids in their $80 dance costumes, let alone up on a stage in front of hundreds of people. But after a year of hard work (the teacher's, that is), they were apparently ready. I was surprised when our dance teacher told me my daughter had learned a routine at all, considering she'd spent half of each week's lesson running out the door to show me her pom poms, wands, tiaras, or just to have a general chat about something irrelevant, until the teacher finally installed a door on the studio.

But apparently she did learn something, because in front of hundreds of people my child did actually walk onto the stage with about 8 other little girls and 1 little boy, and completed quite a bit of her routine by following a couple of older dancers at the wings. Prior to her entrance we had watched a couple of other toddler dances and I had laughed so hard (with loving amusement, not with contempt, I assure you) at some of the little ones that my husband sternly warned me that our child might be even worse. (He has no sense of humour). But I promised him I'd laugh even harder if ours came out and stood facing the side of the stage for the whole number, or sat on the floor trying to peel something off it, or wandered into the middle of another act that wasn't even hers and tried to join in. Because three year olds. All of that actually happened, and I enjoyed it much more than trying to get her to wear her hair clips earlier on.

The dance teacher thanked all the students for their efforts, and for getting up on stage and "doing whatever they choose to do". I can't wait for next year.

Side note: if there's a video of the dance concert available, get it whatever the cost. Your kid will spend hours dressed up in their costume dancing along to it. It'll pay for itself.

My friend: If you don't do as you're told, you won't be able to be four next month. You'll have to stay three, because only good boys grow up.

My friend's three year old: Well then, I'll go back to two. Or one.

K is for....

(Other People's) Kids

It's so funny when someone else's kid is so adorable and beautifully behaved in your presence, and you comment to their parent about how lovely s/he is and the parent says "Oh no, s/he was an absolute devil this morning, actually every morning, well all day every day in fact, and I'm not sure why s/he's being so nice right now but it won't last".

Thank goodness.

On Having a Second….Or More

Maybe I'm a wimp, but NO. JUST NO.

I seriously admire parents who decide to go a second, and especially when their first is still in nappies. I'm not trying to put anyone off here, I'm just putting out my own extreme reservations about having more than one. And as for twins: well, I just can't even imagine. I think the best thing about having twins is that they'd have a playmate, and you might get more washing done if you could leave them amusing themselves rather than taking two whole days to get a single load washed, hung, brought in, folded and away because you are interrupted 1,345 times during 48 hours with wants and needs and absolute must-have-right-nows.

I also happen to know three sets of naturally conceived triplets. You probably don't even have to be a parent for five minutes to know that this would be a real test of endurance. One of those sets of triplets are all boys. They have an older brother, and a younger brother. At one stage, all of them were under five years old. Their parents had the fifth "so the first one wouldn't feel left out his whole life". These are incredible parents. Or they're just showing off.

What about parents who have a second "to keep the first one amused and give them a friend for life"? Run that by some parents who've done this, to establish how many fights they have to break up each day, if that's your reason.

> Me: giving my three year old a light spank for some sort of naughtiness
>
> Her: Do it again! Do it AGAIN!!

The Awesomeness of iEntertainment

Here's a picture of my daughter at two years old enjoying some quiet time with her iPad.

She's had it since she was 18 months old. Don't worry, it's an old model – we're not that cavalier with expensive technology. She's proficient at using it, being able to turn it on, choose an app, interact with whatever she's selected, change apps when

she's bored with it, turn it off and let me know when it needs charging. She's ahead of her grandmother in terms of her iPad skill.

I know many parents have this philosophy of "no technology, ever" or "limited technology time". I don't have any rules at all with technology, and here's why.

This is a list of all the activities my daughter has been involved in at various times in her life starting from 10 months of age.

Rhymetime at the library
Storytime at the library
Art classes
Circus skills
Toddler gymnastics
Swimming
Dance lessons

Martial arts
Toddler music classes
Plenty of play dates

And a couple of days a week at daycare then preschool from aged two and a half.

That's pretty busy, right? Quite active and engaging for one so young? I pretty much sat around, ate and drew pictures for the first four years of my life. I'd say given all the stuff she does, she's entitled to a bit of rest and relaxation sometimes. And if that's what she chooses, it's fine with me.

I do need some time to myself each day too, even if it's just cleaning the kitchen or reading the Saturday paper on a Wednesday, which is when I finally get to it. I don't even know how parents achieved all this before the iPad came along.

There's a human condition we tend to share, and it's known as "give someone too much of what they desperately want, and they'll get sick of it eventually". Turns out it's true for little kids too. At 6:15am when I'm not quite awake and nowhere near ready to get out of bed, I beg my early riser to get her iPad and bring it into the big bed so she can watch it for a while before I get up. And sometimes, she refuses. There I am, begging her to get some screen time, and she prefers to jump all over the bed and make forts while I'm still in it. So the whole "no rules" thing actually backfires on me. It's ironic, isn't it?

Allegedly there's research about children and screen time, too, with negative results. I say, show me an adult aged 30 or over who had too much screen time as a toddler who's now showing long term damage. No one can do this, because there aren't any 30 year olds yet who had too much iPad time when they were three. There are, however, plenty of 30 year olds, and even younger people, who've invented such revolutionary life changers as Facebook, Google, Instagram, Twitter, and countless apps. These young internet prodigies are multimillionaires. Imagine what our three year olds will be able to do if they've actually grown up with the technology?

L is for....

Late

You'll be late for lots of things when you have kids. This is because it will take you so long to get your child(ren) dressed, fed and teeth brushed, that you will sadly pine for how easy it was before.

You'll think you've got lots of time to spare, like for example you have an hour and a quarter to get through breakfast. You could read an entire morning paper in that time, right? Your kid will feed themselves half a Weetbix, one flake every 6 minutes. Then, when time is becoming critical, they will demand that you feed them the rest.

Keeping Your Child Amused

Before I had a child (ie. before I had a clue) I used to wonder why parents didn't carry stuff around for their kids to keep them entertained when they were out and about. I often saw young children bored at cafes, and people used to bring them to my house and let them run about putting drink coasters in their mouths, tipping picture frames over and reaching for decorative items on bookshelves. So when I had my own child to take places, I made sure I had some crayons and paper, or some favourite toys, or a couple of books. And it was then that I finally understood why nobody bothers.

It's because your child is absolutely not interested in anything you have specifically provided for the purpose of their entertainment. In cafés, my child would rather play with a napkin, the fake flowers in the vase or the candle on the table. Or, play with nothing at all, and sit and whine instead. If I set out a piece of paper with some crayons, they are shoved onto the floor. You can see why parents give up.

Here are some ideas for keeping your child amused. They may or may not work. They may work one time, and not the next. I don't know. Good luck.

Activity	Idea
Washing the car	They'll wash the same spot for ten minutes without getting it clean, but kids seem to love washing cars. My car has never been so clean since I gave birth to a little minion to help me out. It's become almost a weekly event and I even buy my child her own car washing supplies like fluffy gloves and microfibre pads on sticks. She can't get enough. And when she has had enough, she likes to jump in the puddles of soapy water or simply walk around the car, telling me where I've missed the dirt, like the bossy boots she is.
Visiting someone's house	It's a tough one, but it depends 100% on whether your host has children or not. If they've had them in the last 25

Activity	Idea
	years, or if they've since had grandchildren, you are A-OK. Just turn up and hope for the best. If you are visiting someone childless, it gets harder. I suggest you make it look like you've made some effort to keep their place intact. If your child is into iPhones or iPads, that's a good start. (Take headphones.) You could also take a DVD or two, one of your child's favourites. Food is a great idea, too, but try not to take anything too crumbly. Maybe take a tarp with you and sit your child on it surrounded by their favourite foods and see how long that lasts. I haven't actually tried this, but it sounds like a great idea, doesn't it? As a backup, you'll need to have a whole bunch of toys they normally like, but be prepared for the chance they'll just not be into it and will instead want to sit on your lap grabbing incessantly at your cup of tea and cake.
Cafes and restaurants	Give them an old wallet and pretend it's yours. Make sure it's filled with old business cards and some sort of plastic cards so you can get them to pretend to pay the bill when you leave (good practice for when they're older).
In the car	Sometimes your child will scream for the entire trip to wherever it is you're going. There is absolutely nothing you can do. You have to drive. Just turn up the radio. One day they'll be driving you around and you can scream at them.
At the supermarket	If you can't justify the extra expense of home delivery, or wait for somebody else to do it, take an old bathmat with

Activity	Idea
	you to the supermarket, and a small pillow. Lay them carefully in a supermarket trolley and entice your child to lie on them "Look! It's a trolley bed! So much fun!" This actually worked really well for me a number of times, even though they tell you not to put your child in the trolley base (stuff that). When they get bored of this, find an open spot where you can swing the trolley around in circles without hitting anyone, or try trolley racing up the aisle when it has something you don't want your kid to see, like soft drinks or chocolate breakfast cereals. As a last resort, you'll have to give them something to eat so they'll let you get through the checkout without a fuss. Just open a box of something you've bought, like muesli bars or little cheeses (but not tampons or cornflakes).
At home	My child loves to go around the house, collect every cushion, pillow, blanket and seat pad she can carry, and then make a big pile on the floor so she can jump into it, pretend to be asleep for two seconds (she's not fooling anyone there) and then jump up, rearrange everything and start again. It used to exasperate me, but the cleaning up afterwards isn't nearly as bad as other things she could be making messes with, like paint, sand or water. So I now actively encourage this activity. I'm looking forward to when we need to replace our next whitegood so I can give her the box for extra amusement.

Toilet Training

In order to prepare you for toilet training, it is necessary to use some immersion therapy. I'm sorry about this. But you need to see it.

This is referred to as a number three, or a poonami.

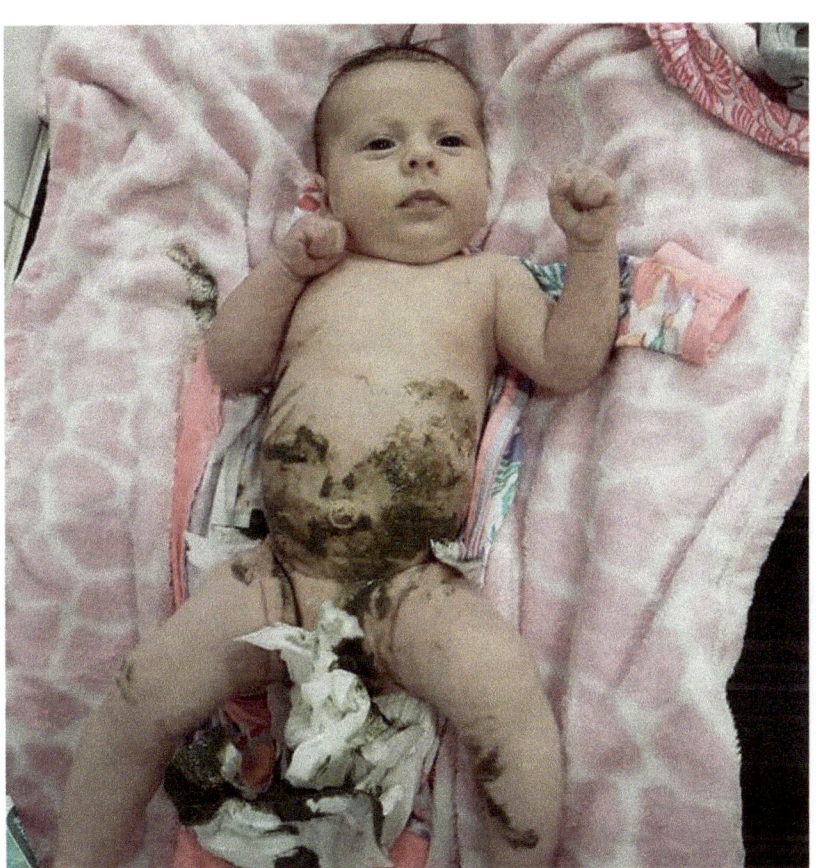

During your darkest days of toilet training, hold onto the memory of this, because nothing could be as bad as this, right?

Just a couple more, so you are sure to remember.

Some parents will speak of their toilet training as if it was nothing at all. "Mine trained in three days at 19 months", they will tell you. "S/he was able to pull down her pants, sit on a potty, wipe and re-dress themselves then continue on with their game of Solitaire without even interrupting me. And they haven't had a single accident since!"

These people are not your allies in the toilet training crusade. Steer clear of them until your child is in school (when, by the way, they might still be in nappies at night. Some kids wear night nappies until they are six or seven. Who knew? I didn't, but there is no room in your life for pressure and judgement from others who managed to toilet train their kids before they could talk. Which, by the way, is far from the average parent's experience).

My child had no interest in sticker charts, promises of rewards, praise for being a big girl, and even (although I intensely hate sugar bribery) chocolate for putting anything in a toilet. After attempting a number of times to get some interest in ditching the nappies, I decided I'd have to join the school of "let them tell you when they are ready".

And at just under three and a half, she finally did. What an exciting weekend that was! It did just happen all by itself within the magic three day period, with a whole day of accidents in the middle but the light dawning on day three and suddenly there we were in Peppa Pig undies, proudly showing them to anyone who would look (she even dacked herself at her grandad's place, so proud she was).

Of course she still needed lots of assistance – she can't always figure her way around her attire, and no one has toilets low enough for a three year old to access, nor a footstool. And little arms can't really wipe properly for some time. There were occasional accidents. Honestly, I'd have been quite surprised if there weren't. After all, it's a serious new skill to master. There are lots of complications.

I briefly became the lucky parent whose child trained herself in three days, and that was that. Or so I thought.

A new development arose, after four mostly successful and drama free months. Ever hear of *toilet training regression*? That's where your kid suddenly forgets what they've learned and decides using the toilet is a bit of a bore. Seemingly unaffected, they will wee everywhere. When you ask them why they aren't using the toilet any more, they'll shrug and say "I didn't hurry?". Obviously.

After the seventh change of clothes and towels to mop up floorboards, you'll think, yay! Now I have enough to put on a load of washing.

Staying calm is the devil during this phase. Try as I might, I often got quite annoyed when my child stood in the middle of the room, let it all out, then pointed to it wordlessly as if to say "here you go. Clean this up now". You are supposed to somehow treat the incident like it didn't happen, but I always ended up being Basil Fawlty not mentioning the war.

> Me: Come on, you have to go to sleep now. We have a big day tomorrow. We have ballet, and then we're going to morning tea.
>
> Miss Two: That's not a big day.
>
> Me: Well OK then, it's a medium day.
>
> Her: It's a small day.

M is for....

Maybe.

It's what you will say lots of times during any given day. It means no. Hopefully your child will take a while to figure this out.

Milestones. WTF are they?

You'll already be familiar with your baby milestones, like rolling over, crawling, smiling, first words, pulling up to a standing position. But just because your child is now two doesn't mean your milestone journey is over.

The trick with milestones is to remember that every child is different and there's no point comparing to other kids (and no point in their parents doing it to you, either). Milestones are valuable mainly if you have worries about your child's development, so here's a handy list of milestones for the toddler to preschool stage that you can absolutely ignore if you want to. I won't mind.

Milestone	Description
Talking	Apparently some kids are conversing about the weather at 15 months, and their worried mothers will be posting on mothers' forums with things like "Advice please? My child is using three syllable words and we are worried that other children his age won't play with him because he's so advanced. Should we take him to a therapist? Also, what schools in our area offer gifted children programs?" Seriously. They learn sentences overnight, so one day they'll have their second birthday saying not much more than mama, dada and poopoo, and within two months they'll be having arguments with you about what they want for breakfast and you'll think how much easier it was pre-verbal.
Dressing themselves	I'm still not sure whether this is a good milestone or not, but the day they start doing it all by themselves

Milestone	Description
	without a single tantrum of frustration and proudly showing you the result is miraculous. It's just that it might take a year or so to get to that point.
Climbing into the car seat by themselves	A personal favourite of mine, I nearly cried with joy when we finally switched to a booster seat and my child got into it with no trouble at about 3 and a half. Both I and her father have had needlework and physio for injuries sustained by repeated carrying of child (me: wrist/cortisone injection, he: shoulder/platelet injection), and twisting her into a car seat did not help matters. By the time she's 10, we might be recovered from our long term sprains.
Toilet training	Covered elsewhere, so all I need to do here is mention that it happens approximately anywhere between 18 months and five years, and night time takes longer. You can stress about it, or you can take the approach that nappies are easier anyway, especially if you're in the middle of Woolworths and you have a full trolley and your two year old has just given you thirty seconds to find a latrine. The less of this sort of situation, the better.
Making friends	The best thing about your kid making friends is that you get to be friends with their parents too.

I've been very lucky here. I've made a whole bucketload of new friends who live locally, and in some cases have even started taking their kids to the same out-of-school activities as my kid, which means I always have someone with whom to trade hysterical sarcastic remarks about parenting while I'm in various waiting rooms at dancing, swimming, or whatever. |

Milestone	Description
	Play dates take a while to "click". Before the age of about three and a half, play dates frustratingly ended prematurely, with our respective children demanding to be on each mother's lap, each of them yelling at us continuously at the tops of their voices and flat out refusing to play with EACH OTHER which was supposedly the whole point; we mothers had so looked forward to sipping actual hot cups of tea and listening to the adorable sounds of our children playing in the cubby house at the other end of the garden. Nope. But, my child has made the most awesome friends with the loveliest little children, and I love their parents too. She did good. I wish you the same.
Sharing	Sharing is nice. Except when it's a runny nose. Parents of only children worry that their child won't learn to share. I have a brother, and as a kid I hated sharing anything. My (only) child has such a lack of emotional attachment to any of her things that she rarely protests when someone touches her stuff. It's genetic (or something) and not related to upbringing (that I can see). Some 35 year olds still hate sharing and they have eight siblings. There you go.
Imaginary play	Warning: You will become involved in this. Imaginary play really means "mummy/daddy, watch me while I pour this imaginary cup of tea into an imaginary cup and then take an imaginary sip and tell me how imaginarily yummy it is". Ad infinitum. Imaginary play should really be called "compulsory parental role-playing with invisible props".

Milestone	Description
Sports	Prepare to become a Dance/Footy/Athletics Mum/Dad, or whatever your child ends up getting into. It's fun. You can form your own Chat Group called Dance Moms, just like the TV show, and you can be relieved that none of you are actually like the Dance Moms on TV. You can all moan about the cost of children's activities, because there's uniforms and tickets and DVDs and costumes and equipment and and and. But the thrill of seeing your kid pick up a tennis racquet a bit larger than they are and give the ball a little thwack is the best thing ever.
Letters and numbers	Prepare to argue with your child about whether a 6 is actually a 6 or whether it's not a 6 at all but really a 5. Even though you have known your letters and numbers for more than 25 years, the wisdom of a preschooler cannot be underestimated. When they look at your clock radio at 6:15am and insist that it's ten thousand o'clock, just agree with them (especially if you're still asleep).
Babycinos	At between $1 and $3 for a tiny cup of froth with a sprinkle of chocolate on top, the sooner your child reaches and passes this milestone the better. I understand cafes need to meet their overheads, but there's something that irks me about recycling the waste product of a cappuccino and passing it off as a gourmet toddler drink. Most of our babycinos have wound up spread across the table, floor or someone's t-shirt, so it's fantastic that my daughter is now sick of them and has moved onto adult drinks like green tea, for which we only have to pay $3 to $5.
Wearing your high heels	I suppose it's practice for when your daughter joins the

Milestone	Description
	corporate world by landing a managerial role at a bank; or for when your son wants to parade in the Mardi Gras.
Jumping in muddy puddles	I blame Peppa Pig for this one. They see a muddy puddle and jump up and down with glee until they are covered in it. I'm not sure whether it was a thing when we were kids, but it's definitely a thing now.
At the movies	It was a big happy day when I discovered that I could take my two and half year old to a cinema and she actually sat through the whole movie without once opening her mouth (ok, so she slept through her first ever movie; but it was a really terrific one so I enjoyed it). Since then I've taken her to at least twelve more (she saw Despicable Me 3 three times) because it's just a chance for me to sit and do nothing. And every time we see a movie, she goes berserk over the popcorn bucket, watches the whole thing avidly, dances to the credits and also the songs during the movie, if there are any. She even likes the crappiest movies (only about a quarter of the movies we see end up suiting my taste). The only downside is that sometimes you can't get mobile phone internet reception inside the movie theatre, which really sucks.
Climbing into the big bed	Just as your child mastering the art of crawling should be met a mix of excitement and a sense of doom that your life as you knew it is now over, your child learning to climb onto your bed should be met with some alarm. You'll now have a regular visitor between 3am and 5am who's ready to party, but first they'll complain that your pillows are all in the wrong place and must be

Milestone	Description
	rearranged. Whether your child will go back to sleep within an hour or so is impossible to say.
Wanting to do housework	So cute, right? Although I find that when my daughter begs to allow me to mop the floor and I set her up with a little rag on a stick and point her to a dusty spot, she straight away loses interest. As usual, give them what they want and they don't want it anymore.
Listening to your music	I was so proud when my daughter started to sing the lyrics to Adam Lambert's Ghost Town. What marvelous taste she has. Unfortunately when your child decides she likes a song, you will find yourself playing it eighty-five times in a row because otherwise they will whine. So make sure you only play them your favourite choices.
Their first hospital visit	This one's a total nightmare. It may be due to an accident, or it may be due to some strange illness or pre-existing condition. Either way, it's horrible and exhausting and you may feel a certain level of guilt depending on why you are there and/or wish you could take every bit of treatment they administer on your child's behalf, but you can't and it's the worst thing ever. No advice here except to cling to the knowledge that the younger your child is, the less likely they'll remember it.
Accidental loss of tooth	Another nightmare, and hopefully another one you can avoid, but if it does happen you have to remind yourself that this one's really common and fortunately the odd baby tooth is dispensable.

N is for....

Not Wearing Enough Clothes

Your child will fuss about having to wear anything warm, throughout the whole of winter. You can show them the snow on the ground through the window, and they will yell "BUT I'M BOILING".

I let my child take a step out the door on a twelve degree day in her singlet, and only then will she let me put her in a hoodie. Five minutes later she'll be pulling it off.

Other People Will Feed Your Children Sugar

There's nothing you can do about it. If you're a parent who's relaxed about your child's sugar intake, or if you are parent who was obsessed with your first child's diet and keeping it wholesome at all times but you've just had your fourth kid and now you don't care, then Kudos to you my friend. I'm still in level one panic mode about keeping my child's daily sugar intake to below two teaspoons, or preferably zero if I can manage it.

So I'll admit it drives me into a furious (although grudgingly silent) rage when strangers, grandparents or other parents offer my child a lolly, chip or biscuit. Some parents keep a bag full of such things for their own offspring – and I get it, I know it's hard to get children to eat properly, and sometimes you have to concede defeat – but that does not mean I will be happy or gracious when they wave that nutritionally devoid stuff in front of my kid's face.

And it really does not help in *any way at all* if people ask me first, pretending to be all conscious of my parenting rules, when they're holding up a lollipop in front of my kid's face. She can SEE you know. She may not know what a Chup-a-Chup is, but my goodness if she sees one, she will certainly want it. She can also HEAR. So if people do care about it, they'd at least spell it out – "can I offer your child a K-I-T K-A-T?" which I will appreciate until she learns how to spell. Better yet, they won't offer us anything at all. I do manage to feed my child most days; she's not starving. If my child sees what other kids are eating and starts nagging me for some, that's my problem and I'll deal with it.

While we're on the subject: Children's Parties. I dread them. I hate to be the parent who isn't going to let her child attend a birthday party every weekend of the year, but judging by the few we've already been to, I may just become that mean mummy. Is it so hard to provide healthy food? I would be thrilled to bring a plate of something tasty and savoury if it's so much trouble. We're not in the 1970s anymore, people. Back then that's what parties were all about, because we knew nothing else. But the sheer range of choices we have for children's parties these days is incredible. You can have a mani/pedi day for your daughter. You can have a Lego party for your son. Or swap them around, if that's what your child is into. It is no longer about stuffing your face with M&Ms, cupcakes, snakes and Fanta.

And finally, parting goodie bags: guess what happens to bags of lollies once they get to our house? In the bin, after I've had the box of Nerds (they are seriously delicious). If I ever get up the courage to host a party at our place, I'm breaking tradition and giving goodie bags with toys and no sweets. It's about time.

> Me: How about you go put your shoes in your room?
> Miss 2: How about no?

O is for....

Observant

Small children are astonishingly observant. They will notice when you wear a new pair of shoes that your partner doesn't know about. They will notice if you shred zucchini very finely and mix it into the lasagne. They will notice if you have a new wrinkle or pimple. They will notice if their noisiest toy suddenly disappears, even if they haven't played with it for 6 months. And they will be very vocal about all of these experiences.

OH FFS

One Day I'll Do A Load Of Washing Without A Fricken Tissue

Mothers' Groups: The Virtual Kind

I tried to join a real mothers' group when my daughter was about 8 months old, but I'd clearly missed the boat. I had no idea you were supposed to join these things immediately after you have your baby, because if you wait too long all the friendships will be formed before you get there and you won't be of any interest to anyone. I know it wasn't about me: there was another newbie mum with an 8 month old at that first and only meeting I went to, and she was ignored too. So I decided to join a few virtual mothers' groups, the Facebook kind. And they were much more rewarding.

You can be a spectator in these groups without feeling like you're being ignored, for one thing. But if you want to be heard, there are thousands of mothers dying to be of assistance to you, and whining about all things parenting is practically a requirement. It can be quite repetitive (see pie chart on the next page) but now and again a gem of information will appear.

You won't be exempt from mummy judgement though. Try posting something a bit controversial or inflammatory and see what happens (just kidding. Don't do it. You're much better off waiting until someone else does, as things can quickly escalate and before you know it Admin has stepped in to break up the fighting and do a bit of admonishing before referring people to the Group Rules. And you might be banned from the group).

(Actually, in some social circles, it's a bit of a badge of honour to be kicked out of a Facebook mothers' group. People will cluster around you, saying "what did you post? What did they say? But that's not fair! No one has a sense of humour any more". And you might even make it into the local paper, or possibly set up a rival Anti-Mothers' Group called "FU, Inner City Mums". You can start making merchandise and a whole new career based on your sarcasm and wit. I'm not even joking.)

Here's a sample transcript from a typical post on a mothers' group page.

Mother: I'm having severe pains in my side. It's been happening on and off for three days. Has anyone else ever had this? What should I do.

Reply: Try some chamomile tea.
Reply: It's defo appendicitis. My cousin had this.
Reply: Essential oils work really well, I sell them. PM me.
Reply: WHY ARE YOU WRITING THIS? GO TO EMERGENCY.
Reply: ^^ This
Reply: Are you getting enough kale in your diet?
Reply: You might be pregnant. Have you taken a pregnancy test?
Reply: I had this years ago and it was food poisoning. What did you eat this week?
Reply: I had this years ago and it went away.
Reply: Why is everyone writing so many stupid things, she needs to go to a doctor.
Reply: No need to be rude ^^
Reply: She's not being rude. It's a stupid post. Someone tag admin.
Reply: Why don't you tag admin?
Reply: While everyone is here, can you look at this pregnancy test and tell me if it's positive?
Reply: I can't see anything. How many days post ovulation are you?
Reply: About 4
Reply: Ok so far too early to tell. You need to wait until 12 DPO.
Reply: But I've got symptoms. My boobs are sore.
Reply: When I was pregnant I knew before I even conceived.
Admin: Turning off comments now. Behave yourselves.

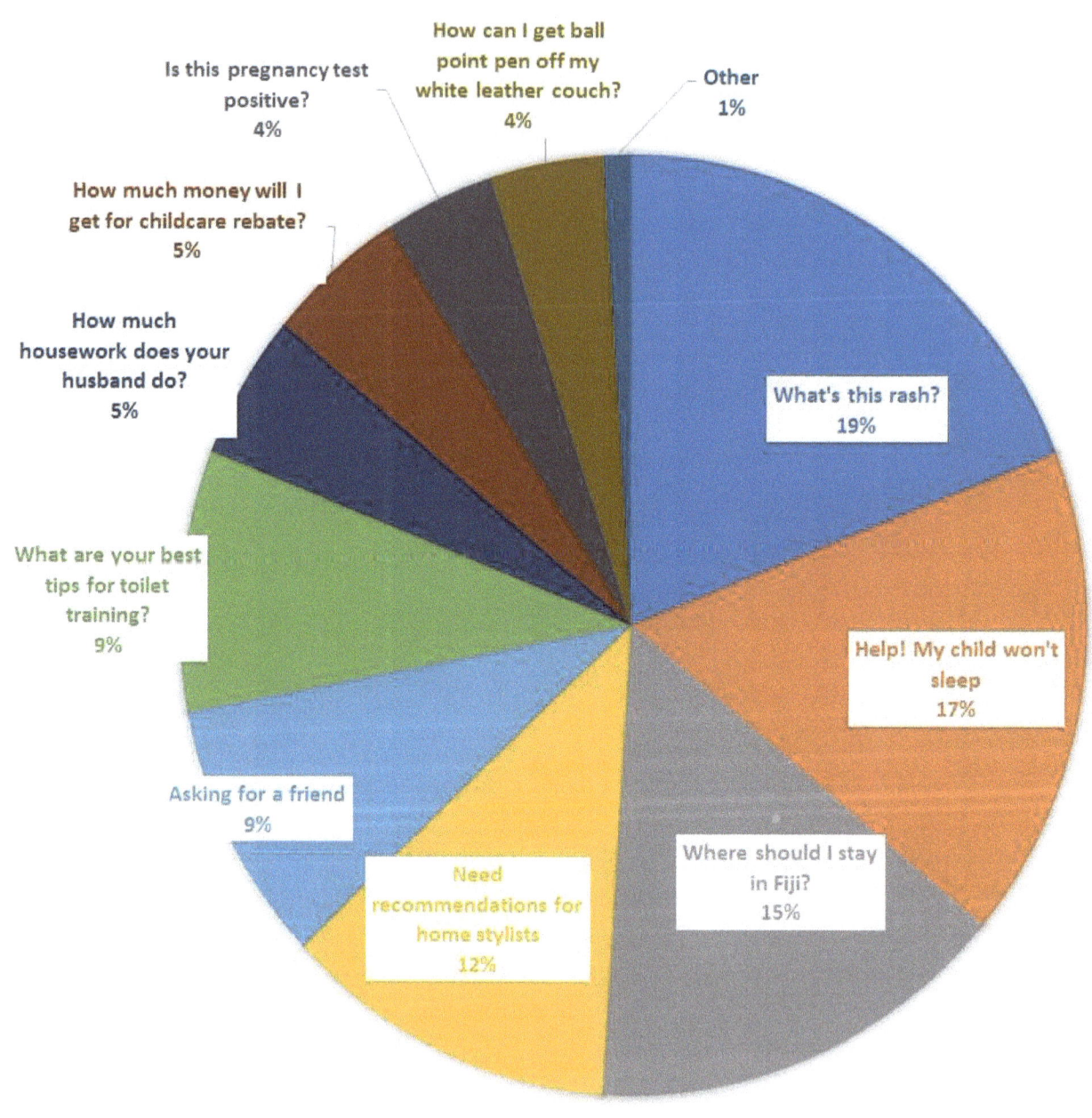

P is for....

Patience

Man, I was full of patience for all sorts of idiots before I had a kid. But now it's gone, all gone.

Dear Parenting Expert

Dear Parenting Expert,

I'm about to start toilet training my 37 and a half month old. How many pairs of underpants should I buy?

A. Oh, anywhere from 50 to 2,500.
PS. Three. Your child is three.

Dear Parenting Expert,

I'm having a lot of trouble getting my son's teeth brushed. He is 18 months old and he makes such a fuss, any tips?

A. Yes indeed. Pin him down on a change table and get the brush in there. Brushing your child's teeth is non-negotiable. The louder he screams, the easier it will be to get the brush in!

Dear Parenting Expert,

I just can't seem to get my house clean. I've got three children and the place is always a disaster. It really depresses me. How can I stop feeling this way, knowing that nothing I do will keep the house presentable?

A. You have three options. 1. Valium. 2. Netflix. 3. Give the kids away.

Dear Parenting Expert,

My 18 month old eats everything I give him. He will try anything I put on his plate, and is always hungry! Spaghetti, ham, chicken, baked beans, kiwi fruit, and any vegetables, even broccoli. Should he be eating so much, should I be worried that he doesn't turn away any food?

A. Don't worry. Your child will soon be two, and then he won't want to eat anything except toast, bananas and yoghurt for at least a year.

Dear Parenting Expert,

My three year old daughter wakes up every morning at 5:30am and won't go back to sleep. We work full time and are exhausted. It's been going on for months and we never get a sleep in. What can we do?

A. It's just a phase. It generally ends after eight or nine years. Just keep looking forward to when your kid is a teenager and won't get out of bed at all. You'll be able to storm into her room before 11am every morning banging a Chinese dinner gong, and jump all over the bed shouting GET UP GET UP GET UP GET UP. You can do this every morning until the day she leaves home. By all reports this won't be for a very, very long time.

Dear Parenting Expert,

My 18 month old was bullied by a two year old on the weekend. They were in a ball pit and the other kid threw a ball into my kid's face. He wasn't really hurt, but I think the parent should have disciplined their child. What should I do next time this happens?

A. Ha ha ha ha ha!

Sorry, couldn't help myself. Look. We are talking about little kids who have many years to go before they develop any sort of empathy for other people, understanding of how their actions affect others, and what it means to apologise for their wrongdoings. If you've managed to teach them this stuff before they turn 18, your parenting job is going well.

But this was a two year old! You don't even have a two year old. Just wait until you do. Then you'll understand.

So what should you do? Stop using words like "bullied" until you are called into school to explain why your child whacked another kid in the nose. Stay out of ball pits if you don't want balls in your kid's face. Smile at other parents who have two year olds – they need it. And if your kid isn't hurt, go back to your latte and your newspaper and stop being a helicopter.

> I'm just watching my four year old sucking her thumb as she plays with the toy her nanny bought her for not sucking her thumb any more.
>
> *- One of many grandparental paradoxes you will experience.*

Q is for....

Quickly

A word your child won't understand until they've grown up and left home.

Things You Said You'd Never Do When You Had a Kid

I'll confess right now that I said *all* of these things before I had a kid. And I'm so embarrassed. How wrong I was.

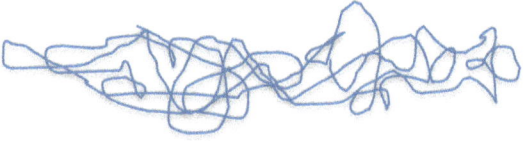

"I won't be letting my kid wear those disgusting Crocs."

No way will I be putting artificial materials on my child's precious foot. Crocs and their imitations are poor excuses for footwear, with inadequate levels of support and ventilation. Plus they are super ugly.

As it turned out, I missed a few things here. For starters, childrens' shoes are expensive. The full leather ones, if you can even find them, will not last long before your kid outgrows them. Even worse, my kid wouldn't even allow them near her feet. I have several pairs of adorable pink leather sandals still in the original packaging, because they would induce a full blown tantrum on sight. (I still cringe when I see them in her wardrobe, because what a waste.) The only proper shoes I can get away with are brightly coloured princess sneakers with Anna and Elsa on them. And of course these are no good for swimming lessons, sandpits, beaches and summer play dates. So = Crocs.

"My kid will have three meals a day, with a snack at morning tea and afternoon tea. And they will never eat in my car."

In my pristine car, and on my spotless couch and floors, children will not munch away on crunchy, crispy things. Not a crumb will lodge itself in the deep folds of my kid's booster seat because that's disgusting. Also, why do people need to feed their kids all day long? What's up with that?

Try feeding your child three full meals a day. Sound easy? After an hour at the breakfast table when my child has eaten two teaspoons of cornflakes during that time, we often have to leave the house to go somewhere. The only way I can get her into the car is to promise her something to eat in the car, because despite spurning perfectly good cornflakes, she's hungry.

Don't try to fight it. Just go with it. And get one of those vacuum cleaners with a long thin attachment for the hose. And get rid of that clean house obsession, it will do you good.

And by the way, there are days when all your child wants to do is eat. Every 18 minutes. Just when you'll think they can't possibly still be hungry, they'll be whining for more. And you have to give them food, because you're their parent and you're supposed to be responsible. So stock up, buddy.

> I have three children. So, basically all I do is feed people all day long.
>
> - *A mother*

"Bribery is unnecessary and you're not a good parent if you do it."

Good grief. Did I really say this? I have a new saying now. It goes like this: "Whatever works". Not only that, I despair that my child generally turns up her nose at bribery. On the rare occasion she will accept a gift in exchange for behavior I'm hoping for, it'll be a once-off.

"There's no need to threaten or yell at a child. They respond much better to calm and rational behavior from the parent."

I can't even type that one out without snickering to myself. The funny thing is, I was very calm and rational before I had a child. I can't tell you the last time I had a temper tantrum pre-kid. Now of course I have them regularly. If you can remain calm and rational while facing your sixteenth tantrum of the day over the fact that there are too many bubbles in the bubble bath, you are a better person than I.

As for threats, well, sometimes that's the only way I can get my child to do anything at all. I can ask her nicely to put her shoes on about twenty times; and she will pretend to be deaf, singing "la la la la la la la" at me; the only thing she's missing is putting her fingers in her ears to mock me. But if I threaten to throw her favourite shoes in the bin if she doesn't put them on *right now* it gets the result. Whatever works.

> Miss Two: Fucksake.
> My husband: *Looks at me*.
> Me: I know. Totally my fault.

"I'll never let my kid do that."

Do what, exactly? What are you not going to let your kid do? Speak rudely to their grandad? Push another child? Throw their toys around? Have a tantrum because you wouldn't buy them a puppy? Run around a café while people are trying to enjoy their morning coffee? Run out onto the road while you turn your back on them for one second to put something in the car even though you've repeatedly nagged them not to? I hate to break it to you, but you can't stop your kid doing any of these things. It's best to accept it's going to happen and try to stop judging other parents as of right now, lest you yourself be judged.

"My kid will behave themselves in public".

Righto.

R is for....

Repeating Yourself

Also called nagging. It's what you said you wouldn't do when you were a kid and your mum nagged you. Now you understand why she did it, and you also understand that she really meant it when she said she hated doing it just as much as you hated hearing it.

Things You Find Yourself Saying After You Have a Kid (that you never thought you'd say)

Come over here so I can smell your bum.

Stop eating the bath bubbles. Stop drinking the bath water.

Stop licking the toilet seat.

Don't put your finger up the dog's bottom.

Do you need the toilet? Are you sure? Then why are you holding your bottom?

Is that chocolate or poo?

Stop putting peas in your ear.

Please stop saying butt crack.

Please stop using my top as a tissue.

Have you pooed today?

I will cut your thumb off if you won't stop sucking it.

Can you please flush the toilet every time you use it?

Why are you scared to flush the toilet?

Ok, how about I flush every time you use the toilet?

I'm going to drop you at preschool on Monday and never collect you again.

Things You Find Yourself Doing After You Have a Kid
(that you never thought you'd do)

Actually getting into the car (without your child) and driving a few metres after threatening to drive off without your child when they won't get into the car.

Finishing food your child has picked over to avoid food wastage, because it pains you so.

Making three separate meals, one for you and the other parent, one for your child, and a second one for your child because they won't eat the first one.

Getting apathetically complacent about bedtime, in the vain hope that if you let your child stay up super late they'll either get really tired and fall asleep easily (doesn't work) and they might sleep in tomorrow (doesn't work).

Using the Broken Record technique to try to get your kid to do something/not do something. It sounds like this: Put your pants on. Put your pants on. Put your pants on. Put your pants on. Put your pants on. Put your pants on. Put your pants on. Put your pants on. Put your pants on. Put your pants on. Until you want to choke yourself.

Instead of being irritated, feeling full of glee and so grateful that the screaming three year old in the shopping centre is not yours.

Volunteering to go to Woolworths on a Saturday morning to do the entire weekly shop because it'll get you away from the house and you can be alone.

Some Things you can do on Facebook to Annoy People

1. Post regular pictures of your growing baby bump, from inception through to bursting point. If it's your second or beyond, make side-by-side collages so everyone can see how big you were at 4 months and 3 weeks during all of your pregnancies.

2. Share the shit out of those Timehop Facebook history posts that pop up in your feed, to make sure everyone remembers what your baby looked like 1, 2, 3, 4, 5, 6 and 7 years ago. Because for sure they will have forgotten.

3. When your baby has a birthday, write a long heartfelt message to them on their big day, even though they don't have Facebook and probably can't even read. Make sure you say things like "To our little darling, we worship the ground you walk on. You are fierce, intelligent, caring, empathetic and the most adoring little sister ever. We can't believe we are so blessed to have your presence around us each minute of every day, and we know you will go on to do amazing things with your life". Even if it's her first birthday.

4. Describe your increase in breast size when pregnant. An announcement like "Wow! From C to E cup 😊" will do nicely. Because everyone needs to know this. And on the same topic:

4a. Breastfeeding.

    Here is a list of people who are super impressed that you are able to breastfeed:
    •
    Here is a list of people who are just dying to see a picture of you doing it:
    •

    And that goes double for celebrities.

5. Hold a birthday party for your kid. Take 287 photos. Put them all in an album on Facebook, even the one of the back of someone's head, or the one of a shoe under a table.

S is for....

Single Parenting

I used to hear reports of couples staying together and actually believe it was "for the children" despite the parents not liking each other very much.

It's not about that. Staying together is "for the parents". Because almost anything is preferable to the difficulty of raising small children on your own.

Hats off to single parents. Don't know how you do it.

#hashtag

In case you use Twitter, or Instagram, or Facebook, or like to drop hashtags into general conversation, here are some you might find useful.

Hashtag	Popular Usage
#assholeparent #assholeparents #assholeparenting #parentoftheyear #parentoftheyearaward	You try to give your child a piece of fruit to snack on. You make them wear a warm hoodie on a cold day. You make them wear shoes because it's raining outside. You try to take a sip of your drink that you are sharing with your child. You won't let them stomp on dog poo. You won't let them eat Vaseline. You try to cut their toenails. You put clean sheets on their bed. You stop them from sticking their fingers into the power socket. You hide all Easter eggs before your kid even sees them. And eat them all yourself. You take your kid to a theme park, and they are beyond terrified by the people dressed in animal suits. Your child gets stuck in the toilet, and you take a pic so you can Instagram it. Your child gets their head stuck in a child's toilet seat attachment and you have to cut it off with actual tools, but first you take a pic so you can Instagram it. You go to Disneyland, without your kids.
#parentproblems #mummyproblems	Your child is upset because you "drowned" the toilet paper You leave the kids with your partner for five minutes

	and everyone acts like you'll be gone for five years Daylight savings starts or ends, and your child's sleep pattern is ruined for months. You have to buy a present for someone else's kid, but you have to take your kid with you to the toy shop. Your kid swears, and you can't stop laughing. You do one thing to make your kid happy, and then you discover that you have to do it 100 times a day now to keep your kid happy.
#sothishappened	You had a baby.
#itstooquiet	Your kid has drawn all over your walls with a Sharpie pen. Your kid has got into your lipstick box and painted the bathroom pink, red and brown. Your kid has covered themselves with Sudocrem. (Here's another free tip. Never, ever leave the Sudocrem within their reach. You're welcome).
#reasonmykidiscrying #tantrum	Your kid's sushi has fallen apart into pieces during the meal. Your child can't tear a piece of paper in half. You gave them a Weetbox that was already broken in half. Your child can't cut their whole Weetbix in half. You made the mistake of taking your child to K-Mart and told them they could only pick out one dress, one tutu, one pair of pyjamas and one swimsuit.
#parentinggoals	Your child slept overnight. Your child slept overnight for two nights in a row.

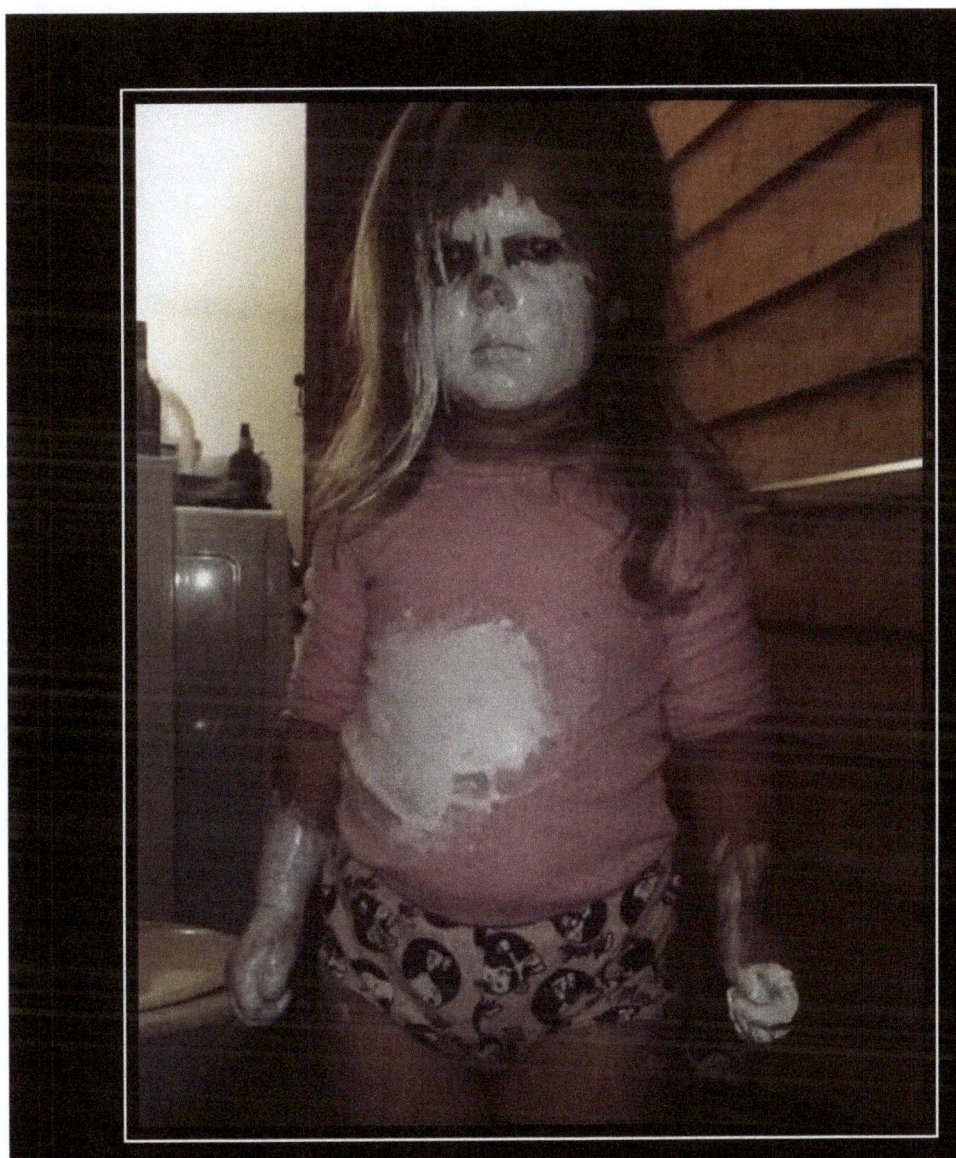

#twitterism

Stephanie Ortiz @Six_Pack_Mom

It's 8:40am & I just broke up a fistfight over who gets the last tater tot, in case you're wondering how fulfilling parenthood is.

Burning Mom @MomOnFire

Tell me again how your unborn child will not see a screen before she's 8. I want to write down your exact words.

> My three year old: I like holidays. I like relaxing and eating jelly.
>
> *(Note: I'm not sure whether she means simultaneously or independently).*

Unfiltered Mama @UnfilteredMama

Overheard my toddler tell her brother, "I not crazy. I two."
Like there's a difference.

Lurkin' Mom @LurkAtHomeMom

Kids: *asking me questions 1/2 inch from my face*
Me: Woah, I need you all to pretend there's like a 2 foot bubble around me.
Kids: *slowly backing away*
Me: Ok. Now. What do you want to ask me?
Mr 7: Can we come into the bubble?

Dad and Buried @DadandBuried

Saying please to a toddler is like being polite to a tornado.

Kerry Wilson @whatbabytalk

Me *switches cartoons off*
Toddler *empties all Tupperware out of drawer, unlocks front door and tries to run out, dumps full container of fish food flakes on floor.*
Me *switches cartoons back on*

> Mummy mummy mummy mummy! What's this?
>
> - My four year old, waving a tampon around in front of a table of guests after digging through my bag. Nothing is sacred when you are a parent.

Robert Knop @FatherWithTwins

*overheard from the other room
8yo: Can I have an ice cream sandwich?
Grandma: Did you finish your dinner?
8yo: No.
Grandma: Just one then.

T is for....

Thumb Sucking

I'm just hoping, as a parent who has tried everything to stop her buck-toothed chronic thumb sucker to stop sucking her thumb, that some awful kid at school next year will taunt her about it and fix in 20 seconds what I haven't been able to do in two and a half years.

Mommy Cusses @mommy_cusses

I'm doing a fun activity with my son which means I'm doing a fun activity by myself while he plays next to me.

Mommy Cusses @mommy_cusses

Today my son saw a box of his old toys I was donating and he said, "What the shit?" and I was like oh. my. god. so you DO hear me when I talk.

dadpression @Dadpression

Baby: Smiles, giggles, and waves at you
Toddler: Tries to break your glasses

Mommy Owl @Lhlodder

Spends 2 hrs refusing to sleep in soft, comfortable bed. Passes out 20 min later, sitting upright, in hard, uncomfortable carseat.

Sarcastic Mommy @sarcasticmommy4

My husband told me to have a good day like he doesn't realize he's leaving me home with his children.

Born Miserable @bornmiserable

I scream, you scream, we've turned into my parents

Mommy Owl @Lhlodder

I hope my kids grow up to be wildly happy and successful people but mostly I hope they learn to sleep past 6AM.

Momsbehavingbadly @badbadmoms

Who are these heroic bitches showing up to school pick up and drop off all showered with jeans on and shit?

Real American Dadass @R_A_Dadass

Welcome to parenthood, if you don't already have high blood pressure you soon will.

> Mummy says I'm a pain in the bum.
>
> - My three year old, to my mother. Cheers for that one, bubba.

Real American Dadass @R_A_Dadass

Taking your kids out for dinner is a great way to remember why you stopped taking your kids out for dinner.

Real American Dadass @R_A_Dadass

Welcome to parenthood, your kid's hungry again.

U is for....

Underwear (Days of Week)

They seem like such a cute idea. Seven adorable little pairs of undies with days of the week on them! Right?

Don't do it. Because on Monday after a rainy weekend, your child will want to wear their Monday undies. And they'll be on the washing line. And they won't wear anything else. And you could just tell them that Thursday undies are Monday ones. But then you feel like a crap mum, because you lied, and your child doesn't read yet but is learning and you're just going to ruin their progress. And Mondays are hard enough already. Just stick with dinosaurs, My Little Pony, Barbie and trucks.

Real American Dadass @R_A_Dadass

Kids are like honey badgers, they don't care what anybody thinks. You want them to spit their toothpaste in the sink, they don't care, they'll spit that shit wherever they want.

Momma's Movin' @Toddler2Talk

If I hear my husband whisper "Go find Mommy" one more time we might be attending a funeral in a few days.

Real American Dadass @R_A_Dadass

Dear toddler,

Sorry I ruined your life when I made you walk because I had a metric ton of stuff to carry and you had 2 perfectly good legs.

Real American Dadass @R_A_Dadass

Kids can make you think crazy thoughts. Like, right now I'm thinking about "accidentally" chopping my finger off just so I can enjoy a kid free night in the E.R.

OneFunnyMummy @OneFunnyMummy

Being a parent is just asking yourself, "What am I doing again?" every two minutes.

OneFunnyMummy @OneFunnyMummy

Mom life is defined as getting 30 minutes to yourself but then having to use it to shave your legs.

Hot Mess Mama @h0tmessmama

I wish I had the confidence of my daughter with her chocolate covered face telling me she didn't just eat chocolate.

The Dad @thedad

Good thing we spent $3.50 on a card for a 4 year old's birthday. I could tell he really enjoyed it.

Sara Says Stop @PetrickSara

The nice thing about being a mom is that instead of being anxious about an upcoming surgery, you can stress over things like how your kid will be getting to practice, or what kind of disaster your house will have turned into by the time you've recovered.

> Miss Three: Mummy, Daddy has a wiggly bottom. Why don't you have a wiggly bottom?
>
> *- Good grief. Don't tell me it's starting already.*

V is for....

Vagina

And P is for penis. Another couple of words you'll be hearing a lot of. Also be prepared to tell your daughter that only boys have penises, no matter how much she wants one, and girls have vaginas even though they're boring.

The Dearth of Good Childrens' Movies

I never used to worry about how good children's movies were. It just wasn't on my radar. I didn't understand what everyone was talking about when they went on about "that song from Frozen". I barely even knew what Frozen was.

Of course, now, I eagerly await the release of a new children's movie with high hopes. I watch television previews very carefully, assessing the storyline, characters, musical score, dancing content (dancing is a winner around here) and the possibility of adult in-jokes. As I've mentioned previously, hardly any children's movies are particularly good and some are horrendous, especially if you have no internet reception on your device in the cinema. Either way, if you have a child who is into movies, you'll be introducing a whole new genre into your movie-going repertoire.

I've also gone back in time via eBay to attain a whole DVD drawerful of children's movies from the past. I can't believe I missed the whole Toy Story thing! Those movies are incredible. Now that I've seen each of them 47 times, I can say with authority that they are some of the best children's movies you can see. The reason is because the creators kept adults in mind when they produced it, and I thank them a thousand times for this. I still cry every time I hear Jesse's song from Toy Story 2, and laugh at the Barbie and Ken scenes in 3. Other movies where adults were thoughtfully included in the audience demographic (because there is a sense of humour, music or other mature theme somewhere in there):

Cloudy With a Chance of Meatballs
Sing
Finding Nemo
Frozen
Moana
Chicken Run
Antz
The Simpsons Movie

Of course there are loads more; I've only considered contemporary animated moves here. But because your child is likely to watch the same movie over and over, you probably only need about 20 DVDs max, which will last you several years. Like me, you'll probably end up singing "When Somebody Loved Me" all day and your kid will be soon be begging you to please stop now.

> Miss Three: Mummy, you've got boobs.
> Me: Yes darling. You'll have them one day.
> Her: But I don't WANT them! I'll look silly! WAAAAAAAAAAAAH!
>
> *- this from a child who wears Peppa Pig leggings, a Frozen t-shirt, a supergirl cape made from a pillowcase, sequined tutu, rain hat, woollen striped gloves and Crocs, all at once.*

Why Your Kid Won't Go To Bed

1. I need a story
2. I need another story
3. I know I had two stories, but I think I need three
4. I need my fan on, it's hot
5. I need the fan pointed exactly at my head. Specifically, my nose
6. I need one more cuddle
7. I'm still hungry
8. I need to go to the toilet
9. I'm not tired
10. I'm missing my favourite toy, despite there being 58 others on the bed
11. Tell me again, what are we doing tomorrow?
12. I just wanted to see what you were watching on television
13. There's a scary monster under the bed
14. I know you checked, but I don't believe you
15. There are shadows on my curtain
16. I know you said it was trees, but I don't believe you
17. I just need one more kiss
18. What are you watching on TV now?
19. I'm still not tired
20. I need a glass of milk
21. A car just drove by our house and it was scary
22. My blanket got all twisted
23. I just needed to know what day it is tomorrow
24. I need some medicine because I was coughing
25. I changed my mind about what I want to wear tomorrow
26. I need two cuddles, three kisses and a high five
27. Now I need a soft high five, and a hard high five
28. Now I need to give you the same
29. Etc.

W is for....

What

What time is it, 5:30am? What are you doing there with that texta? What do you mean, you can't walk up those stairs by yourself? What are you crying about? What is wrong with that meal I just gave you? What do you mean, you ate that whole watermelon and you're still hungry? WTF?

- Me, every day

The Other Great Thing About Caesarians

My four year old has started asking questions about where babies come from, so I showed her a picture of me the day before I was born. After having a good laugh at my huge stomach (she likes to laugh at big tummies) she then asked me earnestly "Where is that shirt you were wearing, mummy? I've never seen that one." And then, after a bit more thought, "But how did I get out of your tummy?"

And it struck me that I have it very easy in answering this question – because I had a Caesarian. I told her the doctor just made a little cut, showed her where, and told her she was lifted right out of my tummy. For some reason she found this entirely plausible, not stopping to ask whether it hurt or how sharp the doctor's knife was or how much blood might have been involved, etc. In fact that was the end of discussion.

Forgive me for not wanting to have the whole sex talk thing with my four year old – for me personally, it's just a bit early. I'm grateful I didn't have to explain how she actually got in there. I'm guessing that'll come when she's five.

> Miss Four: Mummy, can you play me the Leotard Song?
>
> - Meaning, Beyonce, "Put a Ring On It".

My Little Pony and Other Obsessions

Before I had one, I once asked a parent how he kept up with his child's trends and obsessions. Do not worry, he told me. You will ride along with them, as if on a crest of a wave. Boy was he correct.

When your child suddenly develops an urgent and very intense obsession, you will not be able to escape it. It will be everywhere: in all the shops, being worn or carried by all their little friends, in every room in the house and on every channel on television, being spruiked. You'll find yourself having conversations thusly:

Her: We're going to play My Little Pony.
Me: OK.
Her: I'm Rainbow Dash. Who are you going to be?
Me: Erm. Well I don't actually know all their names. Maybe you can decide?
Her: No, you have to pick.
Me: Please… can you help me? What are their names?
Her: Fluttershy. Applejack. Princess Luna. Twilight Sparkle. Spike. Princess Celestia.

(How does she remember all the names?)

Me: OK. I'll be Applejack.
Her: No. You can't be Applejack. He's a boy.
Me: OK. I'll be Princess Luna.
Her: You can't be Princess Luna.
Me: Why not?
Her: Because I'm Princess Luna.
Me: I thought you said you were Rainbow Dash?
Her: I'm also Princess Luna. I'm Rainbow Dash and I'm Princess Luna.
Me: *(in exasperation)* You're really not making this easy for me, are you?
Her: But which one are you going to be?
Me: *(pleading)* Can we stop playing now?
Her: *(firmly)* No.

(Pause).

Her: I really want to be Rainbow Dash.
Me: *(good, we've moved on a bit)* You can be Rainbow Dash, then.
Her: No, I mean I want to BE Rainbow Dash. I want to be able to fly.
Me: Don't we all.
Her: What did you say?
Me: I mean, yes, that would be useful.
Her: But why can't I really be Rainbow Dash for real?
Me: Because you're my little girl. I want you to be my little girl, I don't want Rainbow Dash for a daughter! I prefer you!
Her: But I really WANT to be Rainbow Dash! (starts to cry).

It goes on and on. It started with Lah Lah's Big Time Band and continued with Hey Duggee. Peppa Pig made a strong entrance, then Trolls, and then unicorns. I tried to create obsessions that would work well for me, like wooden train sets, Playdough, Duplo and other toys that would actually require some concentrated effort in building or creating stuff (and give me a bit of time to myself, the holy grail of obsessions). It didn't work – maybe I should have had a boy.

The best $48 I even spent was on a DVD of my daughter's dance concert when she was three. It runs for just under an hour (not long enough, really) and I can often persuade her to put on her costume and dance along to all the songs. It's really cute and I can also do all the steps to the dances now, except the ones where the kids are older than six. Those kids are better than me.

> Mummy. MUMMY. **MUMMY**. I can't find my Emma Wiggle Leotard. It's not in my cupboard. I need you to come and find it NOW. You have to come NOW. NOWWWWWW! WAHHHHHHH!
>
> *- Our house, Sunday mornings, 6:45, awoken by being yelled at. It's like being in the army.*

eXplanations

Your kid will want to know how everything works, where everything came from, why everything happens and why they have to wear a seatbelt. These issues and more, will raise themselves repeatedly even when you think you've dealt with it. See "A", Answers.

Preschool and Beyond

I'm beginning to realise that school is a whole new job for parents, too. (Or, for the parent who does most of the child related administration). They try to ease you into this new job at preschool. For starters, take lunchboxes. There will be a list of things you can't put in them, like nuts, lentils, sesame seeds, peas and eggs. So you have to plan your lunchbox fillings like a military mission.

Then, there's show and tell. You have to provide something interesting for your child to discuss, and if your they're really into it, you need to come up with a different thing every week that can't be a toy lest all the children fight over it. You should probably also not send anything delicate or valuable either. And obviously the same thing can't be sent twice because that's old news.

> Me: You can't take toys to preschool, it's not allowed. And you only get one show and tell per week. Ok?
> Miss Four: Did they send you a note telling you that?
>
> *- I think she's discovered that mummy sometimes makes up rules to suit herself.*

Then there are various events like Halloween (even if you don't live in the USA), Book Week, Mother's and Father's days, Grandparents' day, various other dress up days, school photo day, music lessons, and charity days. Don't get me wrong: all of this stuff is fun and adorable and such. But if you have to be a working parent, it can be hard to fit it all in, or even remember it.

All this is just a warm up for actual school, which will be at least ten times as busy with experiences and activities (but at least there's a school uniform involved, hallelulah – no more arguing over what to wear from Monday to Friday).

I'm already on the mailing list for my daughter's school next year, many months in advance, because I like to be prepared. I'll be recycling our Book Week costume, so that's one thing sorted.

So proud; she wanted to be a toilet instead of some silly princess.

* There's a Big Green Frog in the Toilet, by Anh Do. Thank you for this book Anh, it's perfect on so many levels.

Y is for....

You

You will be a completely different person after having kids. You'll have different friends, different holidays, different family relationships, different priorities. You'll even go to the shops without makeup on.

Some Useful Statistics*
** for the first 4.99 years of your child's life, per child*

Number of hours of your life waiting for your child to get into their car seat	**251**
Amount of wasted food on your child's plate, in kilograms	**24**
Hours spent by your child deciding which top to wear	**197**
Hours of discussions about poo with other parents	**15**
Number of comparisons you will make between your child and other children	**954**
Number of times you will wonder if you have become actually insane	**586**
Number of threats you will make (Times you'll actually carry out the threat)	**3,615** **269**
Cups of tea or coffee drunk cold	**1,837**
Number of times you'll feel like the world's worst parent (Number of times your child will agree)	**7,685** **7,685**
Number of times you'll drop your standards	**5,432**
Number of times you'll say "fuckaduck" sotto voce	**6,731**
Number of times you'll wonder how your parents did this without iPads	**8,349**

Z is for....

Zzzzzzz

The sound of a blissful, uninterrupted sleep, which you may not hear from anyone in the house for a very long time, so I'm just putting it here to remind you of what it sounds like.

One last thing ……..

> Me: (Wearing the same top for the third day in a row)
> Miss Four: Are you wearing that again? (Eye roll)
>
> *- Is that a crime?*

Dedicated to my little darling, who despite all the above

I love more than anything.

www.ingramcontent.com/pod-product-compliance
Lightning Source LLC
Chambersburg PA
CBHW061134010526
44107CB00068B/2930